Morecambe
Back in my Day

An illustrated Memoir by

Stan Henderson

Published in 2024 by Stan Henderson

© Copyright Stan Henderson

ISBN: 978-1-913898-82-3

Book & Cover Design by Russell Holden

www.pixeltweakspublications.com

A Catalogue record for this book is available from the British Library.

Printed by Ingram

Beauty Surrounds, Health Abounds

For

Peter John Henderson

Born Barrow-in-Furness 1962

Died Morecambe 1984

Contents

Introduction

The English invented the Seaside: God created Morecambe!

During my childhood Morecambe was one of the happier places of life. The name itself was enough to conjure up immense feelings of glee, as in – 'We're off to Morecambe tomorrow'.

This book is based mainly on childhood memories, covering the ten years up to 1963 and of times being taken as a youngster to the resort, initially to visit relatives and then later, as a teenager, along with friends, on railway excursions for days out. During the period being recalled, Morecambe was part of the Municipal Borough of Morecambe and Heysham.

Because of a paucity of photographs from the period, some later images have been used where deemed to be appropriate. Digressions, factoids, foreign words, quoted speech and items incidental to the narrative are set in italics.

Originally Poulton-le-Sands, Morecambe had also been referred to over the decades as West Bradford; Bradford-by-the-Sea; Naples of the North and then, rather disparagingly, Costa del Dole, Costa Geriatrica and even Bingo Ville! As the resort grew it eventually subsumed the townships of Bare and Torrisholme.

Despite the slights the place had a magic – it still has! It also has a feel-good factor. Ambling along the crowded front was to be in a sea of smiling faces, with everyone displaying an immense *joie de vivre!* When I became suddenly widowed at the age of 23 I found solace in Morecambe. I could lose myself walking along the promenade. Leaving my car somewhere along

Victoria Esplanade, I would stroll down to the Midland – and then back - pausing to admire the Grand Hotel at the corner of Thornton Road. With its red brick and terracotta gables it was an eye-catching structure. I believe that some buildings, although no longer serving their original purpose, by virtue of their presence, have the ability to make an observer think about their past. From childhood I found I could always appreciate and admire distinguished and noble buildings.

Sauntering along the edge of the bay your anxieties fade away and you are confronted by something fundamental. Being on the seafront allows you to throw off the constraints of time, behaviour, even dress. For a person trying to get a persistent worry out of their head, a walk along here is a wonderful cure. To me it represents total freedom.

Unlike its Lancashire rival on the Fylde, Morecambe in its heyday was not vulgar, having a more genteel atmosphere and a kind of family respectability. Blackpool, that great roaring spangled beast, although bigger, bolder and brassier, did not have Morecambe's panorama of beauty, which had inspired the Romantic painter J.M.W. Turner. For this reason alone the resort stands unchallenged. This book is a tribute to its eminence.

S.Henderson
Haverigg, 2024

CHAPTER ONE

Origins

First of all there was *The Sands* [1], a large indent of approximately 100,000 acres into the Lancashire coastline. Slowly, this 'gulf' went from being the Bay of *Moricambe* to Morecambe Bay. At a point on its southern edge was Poulton (later Poulton-le-Sands), one of three small villages in the area. Lords of the Manor occupied Poulton Hall, a medieval manor house demolished in 1932. Notable families who lived there were the Eidsforths, then the Tilleys. The ancient doorway to the Hall still stands on the town's Poulton Road (Poulton Park).

Morecambe was born of the age of steam. The coming of the railways opened up the area to the rest of the world! A prominent Labour politician once said, "England's coastline is a national treasure. The coast is our birthright and everyone should be able to enjoy it". Morecambe became a place where people came, not to go to sea but to be beside it! During the early part of the twentieth century it could only be effectively accessed by rail. The road from Lancaster, little more than a country lane, came over Skerton Bridge and then *via* Torrisholme. The coastal route (A5105), opened by Lord Derby, which came through Hest Bank, did not come into being until the early 1930s. No longer would holiday-makers, arriving by car from the north, have to muddle their way through Lancaster.

The town had two main railway stations. Each was serviced by rival railway companies. The Midland Station at Northumberland Street was operated

1 The Sands, also known as Lancaster Sands

1

by the Morecambe and Harbour Railway. Morecambe Station – later to be Morecambe Euston Road – was operated by the London and North Western Railway. The NWR ran from Skipton through Ingleton to Morecambe with a connection at Lancaster, to the LNWR between Green Ayre and Castle Stations. At a later date the Midland Station was dismantled and re-erected on the front, becoming Morecambe Promenade Station. Following the 1923 re-grouping, both stations came under the London, Midland and Scottish Railways. (Bare Lane Station was originally called Poulton-le-Sands). As the resort declined in popularity during the late 1950s, with excursions falling away, Euston Road Station closed (1962/63).

Euston Road Station in the days of the London & North-Western Railway
It opened in 1886 as Morecambe Station, with five platforms. It was renamed Euston Road Station in 1924.
Sankey Image Ref: 6294.

It is perhaps ironic (or at least a coincidence), that the current railway halt is in almost the same position as the old Midland Station.

My first visit to the town, I am told, was in 1953. Later, I recall alighting onto a Euston Road platform whilst on an excursion from Barrow-in-Furness.[2] Thereafter, on subsequent visits, I would change at Lancaster Castle Station and board an electric train shuttle to Morecambe Promenade. Morecambe was the first town in the UK to have high-voltage overhead electrification, coming into use in about 1908. The line used to run *via* Lancaster Green Ayre, crossing the Lune over Greyhound Bridge. Carlisle Bridge, during 1963, was being rebuilt. Green Ayre Station was originally used by the old Harbour Railway. It fell victim to the Beeching axe and closed in 1966. Today the site is a public park.

There were two piers, the Stone Jetty possibly being a third? This jetty was part of the old harbour. Up until 1904, when Heysham Harbour opened, steamers plied between Morecambe and Douglas, Isle of Man, also Morecambe to Londonderry from this location. Additionally and until the Furness Railway became properly established, iron ore from the Furness district was distributed *via* Morecambe harbour as it had rail connections to Sheffield and beyond.

The old rail terminus of the North Western Railway, along with the lighthouse, still stands at the end of the jetty.

For many years Ward's Ship Breakers operated from the location of the jetty. The derelict ocean liners awaiting dismantling proved to be an attraction. During the 1920s over 50,000 visitors paid to look over these doomed old ladies of the sea. Ward also broke ships at Barrow and Preston.

The first pier – which became known as Central Pier - was erected in 1869 by Barrow contractor, William Gradwell. This pier was, in fact, second hand, being originally ordered by a South American country, thereby saving the resort thousands of pounds! Following its completion, a celebratory luncheon was laid on at the King's Arms on Marine Road. At some later date this pier was extended, taking an elongated T shape.

2 During the period covered by this book, Barrow was also in Lancashire and like Morecambe is in the Lonsdale Hundred.

I recall that several Morecambe Bay Prawners, with their LR registrations, and other small craft, were moored off this pier.

West End Pier (the second pier) was erected in 1896 and, being almost a third of a mile in length, was one of the longest piers in the country. It was very popular with anglers.

Archie Collis and Ronné Coyles were two local personalities of the Morecambe entertainment scene. I recall seeing their names emblazoned on posters at the

The Old Rail Terminus on the Stone Jetty
Built in sandstone with a slate roof and with a canopy. Grade II Listed Building. List Entry: 1207223.
Photo S. Henderson 2023.

entrance to the piers. Ronné Coyles was a master of tap dancing. On stage this diminutive character, it was said, could mesmerise you! My parents also spoke of an Albert Modley. Unfortunately I have no recall but subsequent enquiries revealed him to have been a popular, all-round entertainer. Mr Modley died at Morecambe in 1979.

I can remember attending shows on Central Pier with my mother and sisters, my father and uncle preferring the *ambience* of the Crow's Nest Bar (nothing to do with the fact that it sold Younger's Scotch Bitter!). The pier manager during these times was the aforementioned Archie Collis, who was also heavily involved with local amateur productions.

Beauty Surrounds

In her absorbing book, *The Seaside*, author Madeleine Bunting says, of the Midland: *Modernist architecture bequeathed many masterpieces on the British coastline – from the famous De La Warr Pavilion in Bexhill-on-Sea to the buildings of Blackpool Pleasure Beach but none, I would argue, matched More-cambe's Midland Hotel. Prominently positioned, it put the town on a par with the most glamorous resorts in Europe. Its architect, Oliver Hill, proudly declared that it was the 'first really modern hotel in the country'.* I had heard polarized views expressed about the Midland, *viz:* 'a building that resembles a clinic for tropical diseases'. I prefer to see it as a part of the Morecambe pageant of loveliness.

By the late 1950s, the Midland Hotel, Central Pier, parts of the front and Euston Road had been the extent of my Morecambe experience.

The Midland Hotel

♫ *If you like the taste of a lobster stew, served by a window with an ocean view. .* ♫
Such was its prestige that French fashion designer Coco Chanel came to visit.
It is a Grade II Listed Building. List Entry: 1208988.
S. Henderson.

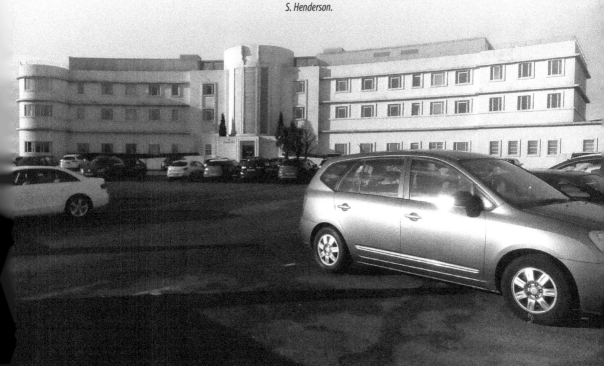

CHAPTER TWO

The 1950s and Schola Green Lane

My mother had three brothers. Frank, the youngest, married Mabel Lillian Collins, a Morecambe girl. Mabel had attended Lancaster Road Primary School and then Euston Road School (one of her classmates had been a certain John Eric Bartholomew). Euston Road School closed in 1973 but its name lives on in the guise of a bus stop. Upon leaving school, 14 year-old Mabel was directed to employment at Creban Manufacturing Ltd. Creban[3] was situated at Westgate Mill, White Lund. They made medical dressings, especially bandages. After having left Creban she was later asked to return as they considered her to have been their best cutter. Mabel went back and stayed until 1964. (My source tells me that such was Mabel's skill in cutting, she had been head-hunted by the firm).

---

3 Creban: probably a contraction of the words crepe and bandage.

Schola green Lane - present day. *Stan Henderson*

Creban Ltd. (Textiles) had been visited some-time after the war by King George VI and Princess Margaret (1951).

Frank and Mabel had met in Morecambe's Tower Ballroom in 1948. During 1949 they went to live with the Collins at Schola Green Lane, a terrace of railway cottages. They wed at St Laurence's Church, also in 1949. The Rev. H. C. Hill of St Barnabas officiated.

Lancashire Post cutting (undated). Creban employee (Nigel Clayton of Heysham) celebrating his exam results. *Courtesy of Janet Clayton.*

Frank and Mabel photographed on West End Pier in 1948. *Courtesy of Patricia Stockton.*

The Collins family, Robert and Lillian, had come to Morecambe from Yorkshire sometime after the Great War. Mr Collins worked in the railway goods yard. Lillian was a widow when my cousin Pat came into the world. She lived with her sons, Frank, John and Robert Jnr., all railway workers. My earliest recollection of visiting was the egg and chips that Ma Collins would make for us. After having made the chips she would always fry the eggs in the chip pan. This gave them a nice golden crispy corona. Mrs Collins was a good cook who was always baking. The main shopping area was Poulton market and along Euston Road where most commodities could be sourced. Redman's grocery on Euston Road (one of three shops later absorbed by JD Wetherspoons) was the main outlet for home baking items where goods were displayed loose and then weighed-out.

The Tower (1953), a couple are crossing the bridge from Central Rockery (left); the corner of Eidsforth Terrace is on the right: Morecambe Postcard Museum, *courtesy of Patricia Stockton*.

The Collins' home at number 47 was surrounded by the railway. Looking over the wall to the west was Euston Road Station, to the east was a mass of sidings. Schola Green Lane in those days was a dead-end to traffic but pedestrians could continue via a crossing, beyond which Schola Green Lane continued.

Frank Stockton was a merchant seaman when Pat, his daughter, was born. He was employed by British Rail, Marine Division and based at Heysham Harbour. Upon settling in Morecambe, he was discharged from merchant service in 1949. Then, after a spell working as a labourer, he took a job with Ribble Motor Services, initially as a conductor and then, from 1952, as a driver being employed as a coach driver (excursions).

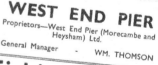

Ribble Motor Services was possibly the largest bus operator in the North-West. Based in Preston, Lancashire it was established in 1919 just after the end of the Great War. Ribble provided a top-end service to the travelling public. Most of the fleet (red buses) were Leylands. I remember they were always a smoother, quieter and more comfortable ride than their corporation counterparts. Obviously more money was invested in suspension and coachwork - they also had nicer seats. Ribble's bus station at Morecambe was on Euston Road, within the curtilage of the railway station.

My uncle, Frank Stockton (hereinafter Frank), was an interesting character with many interests and hobbies. I think the modern term to describe such a person is multipotentialite. Upon reflection, I wish I could have spent more time in his company. He was a collector, a musician (self-taught), model maker, raconteur and a fisherman. He also possessed good business acumen. I think his first and main interest was possibly fishing. Most of his spare time during the 1950s was spent fishing from West End Pier.

Frank fishing from West End Pier, early-fifties. *Family photo, courtesy of Patricia Stockton.*

WEST END PIER

Proprietors—West End Pier (Morecambe and Heysham) Ltd.

General Manager - WM. THOMSON

Fishing Permit

(FEE 10/-)

This Permit Admits the Holder

Name *y⁴ Stockton*

Address *13 Ullswater Ave*

to the Pier for the purpose of Fishing during the Period

Oct. 1st, 19 *58* to March 31st, 19 *59*

Fishing from the Pier can only be allowed between the hours of 8-0 a.m. to 10-30 p.m.

This Permit is Not Transferable.

Ribble personnel stood by an excursion coach. Frank Stockton is on the right. *Family photo.*

Two Morecambe Ribble bus crews relaxing on a bench in Euston Road, mid-fifties. *Family photo*

Ribble's Leyland Leopard. A 40-seater, Continental-Style, coach with Leyland chassis built by Duple Motor Services of Blackpool. Ribble Staff Bulletin.

Driver F. Stockton (Morecambe)
Mr. R. Thornton, of Lancaster, writes :

"I have this day returned from a day coach tour to Carlisle, Gretna Green and the Lakes, and having enjoyed myself so much, I don't want to let it pass without paying tribute to the kindness, consideration and general helpfulness of the driver who so ably drove us there.

The information about points of interest, the little bits of history, even his choice of stop for morning coffee, etc., all added up to make what could have been just another day out, something really enjoyable and memorable. This is the second time it has been my good fortune to travel with him — I think it was last year that he took us to York and Knaresborough, and that journey too was made just as interesting.

So often it is just a case of getting you there and back, but this young man has the ability and obviously the desire to ensure you enjoy your day.

On behalf of my wife and myself I wish it to be known that his efforts are appreciated."

Ribble Staff Bulletin, Feb. 1959. (Single-Decker at Arnside).

Cutting from Ribble's in-house Staff Bulletin.

Ribble ceased operation in 1988 and although absorbed into the Stage-coach Group, their quality, high standard service has been lost for good.

Morecambe town council operated a good municipal bus service between 1908 and 1983. Their depot was at the West End on Stanley Road. During the late 1960s, as an apprentice at Barrow shipyard, I became good friends with a Morecambe lad, Tony Booth. Tony was not sand grown, having been born in Leeds then brought to Morecambe as a child. His apprenticeship was served at ICI Heysham. The Booths lived on Stansey Avenue. Tony was a first-class piping draughtsman and my first dealings with him were in this regard. We got on really well together, both having the same sense of humour. He had been a conductor on the corporation buses during the summer season of 1962. This was around the time that AEC buses were being replaced with Leylands. In 1968 Tony married Jean Henderson, a Morecambe lass. Jean's parents ran Henderson's Chippy on Regent Road.

Part of Tony's job as a conductor was to make announcements so that passengers didn't miss their stops. I remember asking him if it was true about conductors announcing, when approaching the East End and Happy Mount Park, "the next stop is for Bare people?" He replied with his trade-mark wit, "some did, I believe, but I called out – "The next stop is for Bare people who, upon leaving the bus, are to run into the park and get happily mounted!"

Tony told me how physically demanding the job was in those days, especially during the summer season. Running up and down the bus stairs certainly kept his weight down.

Tony had been supportive during my dark days in the early 1970s. For a while I was saddened when he left to start a career in the Merchant Navy.

Morecambe's double-deckers started to be phased out in favour of one-man operated single-deckers from around 1969.

Quite often, during the summer of 1958, Frank would visit my mother. This would be when one of his excursions had brought him to Barrow. He would have left his passengers at either Biggar Bank, Walney Island or Furness Abbey. We lived at Hood Street in Hindpool in those days. Frank would park his bus on Anson Street and then walk across the waste ground to our back door. I recall the following visit only because he had brought me a bus driver's peaked-cap, which I had been pestering him for. As was usual, I would be playing in the back street when he arrived.

"Here, Stanley, go and get me ten Park Drive and then mind no-one touches the coach," instructed Frank as he handed me a two-bob bit. I ran off in the direction of our local shop while Frank went indoors. His visit on this occasion, I was to discover later, was to make arrangements to borrow dad's boat for a fishing expedition into Morecambe Bay with his angling group. Returning with his purchase, I handed him his cigs and change. "Here you are Stanley," he said, handing me his hat. "Perhaps I'll get some peace now?" he chortled. Elated, I ran off sporting my gift.

Another of Frank's visits I recall was around two years later, possibly in 1960 and on a week-end. On this occasion Frank had called to show us his new car, an Austin Somerset. The visit was memorable because when he set off to go home his car wouldn't start! I remember dad looking under the bonnet and diagnosing a faulty starter motor. It being a weekend there were no garages open and Frank appeared anxious. It was clear he didn't want to go leaving his new car in Barrow. Dad offered to tow the car to Morecambe – which pleased my uncle. An old piece of rope was retrieved from our boat store at Ferry Beach and, with both vehicles connected, we set off for Morecambe. Proceeding along Barrow's Abbey Road and at the junction at Station Approach, our trusty tow-rope snapped, leaving us blocking both carriageways of the town's busiest crossroads! Dad jumped out of our car and effected a temporary lash-up, allowing us to ease the congestion. Eventually we were on our way and without further ado, in just over an hour, arrived in Morecambe.

In 1960 the Stocktons moved into one of the new houses on Ullswater Avenue, then in 1964 they departed the UK to start a new life in New Zealand.

The Stockton's family car, a 1952 Austin Somerset Saloon. *Wiki Commons.*

Morecambe Corporation bus emerging from the Stanley Road Depot. *Morecambe & Heysham Past and Present (D. Wharfedale).*

Morecambe saucy postcards. Bamforth & Co. Ltd. Holmfirth, Yorkshire. *F. Stockton Collection courtesy of Patricia Stockton.*

CHAPTER THREE

Middleton Tower Holiday Camp

Towards the end of the nineteen fifties my grandmother, at the age of 65, secured a position as chalet maid at Middleton Tower[4] Holiday Camp. I feel confident saying this was prior to the site being acquired by the Pontins Group. I recall visiting her there on several occasions. We would catch the Heysham Village bus outside the Floral Hall then, after a ten minute ride, alighted near to the junction of Heysham Road and Middleton Road. Holidaymakers who were going to stay at the camp came either in their own transport or on one of the sharries[5] that ferried people from the railway station. There was no public transport direct to the camp. On

Middleton Tower(s). Historic England List Entry: 1164309. Origin unknown; described by English Heritage as a folly.
Courtesy of David Dixon; licenced for reuse under Creative Commons Licencing.

---

4 **Middleton Tower:** not to be confused with Middleton Towers, a Listed Building in Norfolk.
5 **Sharry:** (phonetic), short for *charabanc.*

occasion, horse-drawn landaus were seen but such luxury was beyond our budget. It was a long walk from the bus stop. Crossing the Port road (A683) we would proceed along Middleton Road then turned right in the village onto Carr Lane. Finally onto Natterjack Lane. The entrance to the camp was impressive, nay, *splendiferous*! The approach, along Natterjack Lane, was a single-lane tarmac gradient with several sleeping policemen. It was lawned on either side and interspersed with flowerbeds. There was a row of standing stone piers, painted brilliant white, each stone bearing a letter of the camp's name. Hanging baskets hung from the lamp standards. The camp approach was a vibrant splash of colour! At the top of the gradient was the security barrier, behind which was a line of flagpoles. At the barrier stood a uniformed security officer. On my first visit I thought I was going to meet the Wizard of Oz!

The holiday camp at Middleton Sands, an enormous venture at the time, was opened by Blackpool businessman, Harry S. Kamiya, with a something-for-everyone formula. It became Middleton Tower Holiday Camp and opened in 1939 but was then promptly requisitioned by the government. The Second World War frustrated Harry's leisure project until the late 1940s. Following Mr Kamiya's death in 1952, it was run by his family (his widow, together with another lady). There is conflicting opinion about just when Pontins took over the ownership of the camp. I have seen the year 1955 given but also 1964 recorded. What I can categorically state is that during my visits there was no Pontin's signage, nor corporate Pontin's imagery whatsoever.

The entire holiday park had been professionally planned and landscaped. A duck pond stood at the forward end of the *Berengaria*. This, together with the rose gardens, represented 'a little piece of heaven on earth'. I can fully understand, from my present position, why groups of people would sit wiling away the hours among those lovely plants and flowers. They, like me, probably came from urban terraced or even back-to-back housing.

The camp was located on a 60-acre site next to a 'private' stretch of beach. It comprised almost 900 chalets; dining halls with a combined capacity for 3000; an outside swimming pool; a separate theatre and a kiddie's theatre; the Rendezvous Café and a country pub. This 'country pub' had originally been a seventeenth century farmhouse. It is a Listed Building (Historic England List number: 1071770). This building, along with the eponymous tower, was a feature of the camp. The main entertainment building was contrived to resemble the superstructure of an ocean liner. The interior had genuine *art deco* flourishes. This building featured a bar (Wonder Bar), a restaurant and a theatre. Named after *RMS Berengaria*, it was adorned with several genuine ship's fittings, with the aim of providing guests with an authentic maritime ambience. Such splendour!

RMS Berengaria, originally SS Imperator, was built in the Imperial Germany of 1912. After the Great War and having been requisitioned by the US Navy in reparation for the Lusitania, it was bought by Cunard. She later became the company's flagship and renamed Berengaria. She was, without doubt, the last word in ocean-going luxury. In 1935, having been converted from coal to oil, she set a record for her passage from Southampton to New York.

The ship was retired in March 1938 and finally sailed from Southampton to the Tyne for demolition at Jarrow. Her fittings and furnishings were auctioned in January 1939. Many of which were purchased by Harry Kamiya for his new holiday camp.

The client base at the camp was the 'British Standard' family of the period, as can be seen from the many picture postcards that were issued. Looking back from my present standpoint, I am amazed at how fashions have drastically changed between then and now! To all intents my time at the camp was spent alone, my nanna always seemed to be working. This didn't perturb me in the slightest. I was a people watcher. I would fill my time observing others enjoying their holidays. People wore proper clothes during those times, no trainers, tracksuits or baseball caps – and certainly no loud T shirts! However, the vagaries of fashion do not stand up to scrutiny. In my experience, people have always railed against being uniformed, be they adults at work or children at school. This is why non-uniform days are so popular. But what do folks wear on these non-uniform days? Trainers, tracksuit bottoms and loud T shirts! A different kind of uniform?

The family unit, during the 1950s, was still the institution that underpinned civilised society. Middleton Tower Holiday Camp provided an excellent holiday experience in a safe environment – especially for children – to which I can attest. I don't recall seeing such as blue-coats but there was a team of 'uncles' and 'aunts' who looked after us.

Picture Postcard from Middleton Tower Holiday Camp. *Glen Fairweather Collection.*

I visited the camp several times between 1958 and 1961, mainly as a day visitor. I enjoyed spending time with my nanna – she would always let me wear my jeans on Sundays!

Somehow my nan had secured approval from her supervisor, allowing me to occasionally stay in her chalet. I recall having my very first taste of Coca-Cola at the camp, which was sold in the iconic glass bottle. It so gassed me up that I had belly-ache for hours afterwards! Meals were substantial but only basic (We had never heard of pizza or chicken tikka masala). Tomato soup; liver and onions or sausage and mash, followed by rice pudding or Manchester Tart seemed to be the standard fare. I ate my meals either in our chalet or the staff dining room. (Whilst day visitors were made welcome at the camp, they were subject to certain restrictions and no-go areas).

One of the highlights of my time at the camp was watching the judging of the Miss Great Britain Beauty Competition. I don't recall the actual year but I do remember it was being televised for the weekly TV show, Holiday Town Parade. In this particular year, Middleton Tower had been chosen as an alternative to the Super Swimming Stadium. Holiday Town Parade, was presented by Macdonald Hobley.

Greetings from MIDDLETON TOWER HOLIDAY CAMP

Picture Postcard from Middleton Tower Holiday Camp. *Glen Fairweather Collection.*

Hobley (uncle Mac when on the radio), was of the old school. He appeared in the 1960 film – *The Entertainer*[6] where he reprised his role of beauty pageant presenter. Holiday Town Parade was a regular summer fixture on Saturday night television. It was extremely popular, attracting a viewing audience of around 20 million viewers. In addition to the Miss Great Britain competition, the camp staged its own, junior beauty pageant where the winner would be crowned Miss Middleton.

A very popular song I recall, which was played regularly in the ballroom by the resident band, was the Dorothy Squires hit *Say it With Flowers*. It was also the choice of many of the talent competition hopefuls!

Although my family were not devoutly religious, dad always insisted that Sundays were respected. The school I went to was a Church of England establishment, moreover my sisters and I regularly attended Sunday school in those years. At the camp there were several options for Sunday worship. My grandmother, a Salvationist, occasionally attended services at St Peters, Heysham. She fell in love with that headland. I recall her singing the following to herself, to the tune of an old Michael Holliday song:

♫ *If you spend the evening then you'll want to stay,*
watching the sunset on Half Moon Bay ♫

I often wonder, from my present standpoint, what took Harry Kamiya to such a remote, unspoilt, part of the Lancashire coast in the 1930s? He was obviously inspired by what he saw – his rainbow's end perhaps?

---

6 **The Entertainer** was shot largely in Morecambe. It starred Lord Olivier and Morecambe's most famous daughter, Dame Thora Hird.

CHAPTER FOUR

1963 and Halcyon Days

Despite my earlier perambulations around the resort, I was about to discover the real Morecambe. I was, however, totally unaware that by 1963 it was into its decline!

Twice per month, on Saturdays, starting in the summer of 1963, we[7] would head for Morecambe. Catching the 12.20 from Barrow Central, a corridor train usually hauled by a black five, we would arrive at Morecambe between 1.30 and 1.45pm. Unwittingly, we were about to establish a routine that would continue for over two years!

Once, maybe twice, that year we went to Morecambe on a British Rail excursion. These trips usually left Barrow at 1pm on Saturdays and, after stopping at Dalton-in-Furness and Ulverston to pick up passengers, went straight through to Morecambe Euston Road (possibly the last to do so?).

The return half-fare in 1963 was 2/10d., which equates to about 12 new pence. We each had around £2 spending money in our pockets. Arriving at Morecambe's Promenade Station our excitement must have been palpable! Looking back, and apart from the buzz of the crowds and music, I believe the lack of industrial ugliness would have contributed to our genial love of place. No works' hooters, no smoking chimney stacks and no long black factory buildings. How could such a place of fantasy, magic and adventure be only an hour away from our drab home town? Exiting the station *via* its grand and spacious concourse, and probably pausing to 'eyeball' the recently

---

7 'We': chums John Baker, capstan hand; Mike Boardley, delivery boy (Co-op milk) and Ian Widnall, apprentice painter.

'Pablo's Terrace' with diners outside Rita's Café in 2023. *S. Henderson*

installed milk vending machine, which was advising us to *Drinka Pinta Milka Day*, we would make a beeline for Pablo's Cafeteria[8] and fish and chips. The offering there was both good and plentiful. Just fish and chips (we always asked for whale and chips, which amused Romeo[9] our server). I don't recall seeing such as burgers or chicken being available, although at a later date Holland's pies went on sale. The tables in Pablo's were just big enough for four people and, being Formica topped, they were easy to wipe clean. *I have been unable to ascertain just when Pablo's became established in Morecambe. As early as 1948 there were two Pablo's on the front at Blackpool.*

---

8 **Pablo's Cafeteria** was at 205 Marine Road Central. It shared the address with a rock emporium. It is currently occupied by Brigg's Shoes.

9 **Romeo:** I think his second name was Pye. He told us that his brother was in charge of the donkey rides.

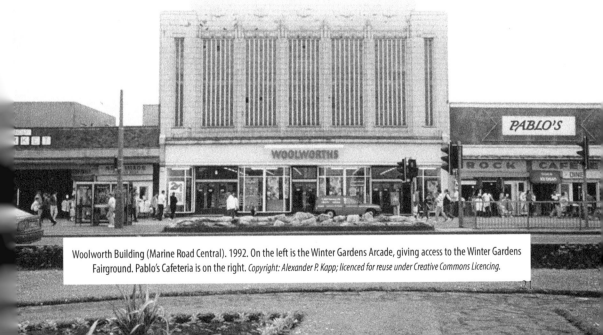

Woolworth Building (Marine Road Central). 1992. On the left is the Winter Gardens Arcade, giving access to the Winter Gardens Fairground. Pablo's Cafeteria is on the right. *Copyright: Alexander P. Kapp; licenced for reuse under Creative Commons Licencing.*

All along 'Pablo's terrace' there would be crowds of people playing bingo in the open-fronted amusement arcade. A man with a hand-held microphone would be calling the numbers in between barking at passers-by, inviting them to try their luck. On the wide pavement along this stretch were exotic looking candy-striped kiosks; a hot-dog stand; a candy floss stall and Madam Petulengro, clairvoyant to the Stars – all doing good business. Lettered More-cambe rock, kiss-me-quick hats and a variety of tacky paraphernalia was on sale along the front, in what we called grockle shops. People could also purchase jugs of tea or hot water to top up their Thermos flasks to take onto the beach. It is recalled that Morecambe-themed tea towels were also available everywhere. All along Marine Road there were open-top buses, trams, excursion coaches, horse-drawn landaus and four-wheel cycles as well as the everyday traffic. On one occasion a stream of Lambrettas told us the Mods had arrived!

On one particular occasion I recall, Ian, one of our group, tried his luck with the fortune-teller. Having crossed her palm with silver, she gave him a detailed account of his future, concluding with the prophecy that in late middle age he would move to Australia, where he would eventually end his days. Ian pondered this then asked, "So if I keep away from Australia, then by your logic, I should live forever?" The mystic was lost for words!

Inside Pablo's we would make our purchase and then dine inside the cafe-teria.

The only other place I can remember having a sit-down meal was in Hart's Crescent Café. We had arrived in Morecambe, accompanied by our fathers, to appear in front of magistrates. This was for the heinous crime of alighting the train before it had stopped. Such was the excitement of coming to Morecambe! This was in 1965: we were each fined the sum of £1.

Having eaten our fish and chips, we would be faced with a choice. Do we head towards the West End Pleasure Park or do we visit the Winter Gardens Fairground? Invariably we would head east, saving the main funfair for our evening jaunt. Nourished, we left Pablo's to agree upon our afternoon's itinerary, after which we would just stand on the pavement taking in the spectacle surrounding us. All human life was here! Continuing along Marine Road, we passed Woolworths and Littlewoods, arriving at the Winter Gardens Complex and the entrance to the *Parisian Bar*. This bar was actually located in the basement of the Empress Ballroom and was accessed down some steps from the pavement. Once inside we were awestruck! The place was massive. The actual bar was at the opposite end of the room to the entrance. Unfortunately, my memory doesn't extend back far enough to recall the décor, which I suspect was a French theme. Waiters in starched white shirts and bow-ties scurried around with trays of beer. Beer, as in most of the Morecambe pubs, was served up in dimpled beer mugs. These were quite heavy so a tray of five or six pints would have been a considerable weight. When the keyboard player launched into that 'sweetest of songs', *Song of the Clyde,* we probably looked at each other in agreement, this must be the Scottish holidays – we were most likely the only Sassenachs in the place! Eventually we managed to get served – Cokes all round.

> *The keyboard player, an organ on this occasion, was probably Morecambe's own, aptly named, Ronnie French. Ronnie was a sand grown jazz pianist of renown. I recall seeing his name, along with Winston and his Hawaiian guitars, on a poster in the foyer of the Winter Gardens. On subsequent visits Ron would be into his jazz repertoire – which our immature tastes wouldn't have appreciated.*

The beer available in Morecambe at the time included Dutton's English Ales; Mitchells, which was brewed in Lancaster. Sam Smith's Taddy Ales; Yates and Jackson and Youngers Scotch Bitter. Lager was available in bottles, draught lager had not yet come into prominence.

Yates and Jackson Ltd were also Lancaster brewers. Their premises were at The Old Brewery on Brewery Lane. As well as the Joiners Arms they had the Ship Hotel (also on Queen Street) and the George Hotel on Lancaster Road. In 1984 the concern was acquired by Thwaites & Co. being later sold to Mitchells of Lancaster, who brewed there until 1991. The average price for a pint of ale in 1963 was 1/3d. This meant that one pound could buy you sixteen pints!

At a later date we were to learn that the *Parisian* had been the resort's first, unofficial, gay bar.

Part View of the Winter Gardens Ballroom, at pavement level, showing the entrance to the Parisian Bar. In the above image it seems to have been subdivided into a Dixieland Bar and a Coral Reef Bar. Access to the ballroom was through the door on the extreme right. c. 1970. *Lancaster Guardian (B. Marshall).*

Having soaked-up the atmosphere of the *Parisian Bar,* we would move on. Emerging back onto the pavement, which would be aswarm with fun-seekers, our attention was grabbed by the pirate ship berthed opposite at the stepped sea wall. Crossing the busy promenade, we were soon at the vessel's gangplank. I have always had a fascination with ships and boats which has continued throughout my life. It was, therefore, essential that I, along with my friends, should look around this old sailing vessel which, I was soon to learn, had featured in such as television's *The Buccaneers* and John Huston's classic film, *Moby Dick*. Paying our sixpence admission, we clambered aboard. We stood for a while on the quarterdeck, simply surveying our immediate surroundings gazing at the doors that led to the captain's quarters and probably expecting Captain Ahab (Gregory Peck) to make an entrance as in the classic film! Our excitement probably got the better of us and we were soon disporting ourselves, acting out a scene from the *Buccaneers*. For a while we were the crew of Dan Tempest's *Sultana*. Having spent some time prancing around on the ship's open deck, we next went below and were surprised to find that there was absolutely nothing to see there! It was poorly lit and a bit smelly if memory serves. It was also surprising, and

disappointing, to see that it was not compartmentalised, *i.e.* no cabins or crew quarters. It was just a large void space. One would have thought that such an attraction would have comprised something like a mini-museum, with artefacts that someone like Harry Kamiya would have provided had he been the owner! Nevertheless, we would visit the *Moby Dick* on every subsequent Morecambe visit.

Moby Dick. Viewed from the entrance to the Parisian Bar. She was moored at the stepped sea wall. In his 1990 book, *Lost Resort?* Roger Bingham refers to the ship as 'the Moby Dick floating museum'. It was not a floating museum in 1963/64 – Author. *Photo courtesy Barrie Marshall*

Several years later I was saddened to read in the local press (1970) that the ship had been destroyed by fire, so I looked into her history:

> *The three masted schooner Moby Dick was built in 1887 by Nicholson and Marsh of Glasson Dock. As launched she was named Ryelands.*
>
> *After having several owners, she was bought in 1929 by Robert Gardner, a Lancaster ship-owner whose business was based at St. George's Quay, Lancaster. An engine was added in the same year. The vessel was Gardner's third largest ship. It had a registered tonnage 123 net and was used to carry bulk cargoes such as grain, sand, stone and coal between west coast ports.*
>
> *In 1942 the Ryelands was sold on and was fitted with a new engine. After passing through the hands of three more owners, she was acquired by RKO/Disney Productions, becoming the Hispaniola in the film Treasure Island. After a period as a tourist attraction at Scarborough, she was back in front of the cameras on the high seas, this time as the Pequod in John Huston's Moby Dick.*
>
> *In 1961 her final berth became the eastern-end of the Super Swimming Stadium, Morecambe.*

It is noted that for each of her 'starring roles' the vessel had her topsides reconfigured to fit the part.

The Moby Dick's hull was painted a light blue, reminiscent of the large wooden drifters/seiners that fished out of Whitehaven during the 1950s. The loss of this vessel was, for me personally, as significant as the loss of the Super Swimming Stadium.

> *In hindsight, certain questions come to mind, such as: When the Moby Dick was opened as an attraction, why was the public allowed below deck? There was nothing to see there! Why were giddy teenagers (such as my group) allowed to roam unaccompanied? Why weren't 'No Smoking' signs posted and why, as she was a wooden structure, were there no*

smoke alarms and fire extinguishers? The interior of the vessel would have made an ideal mini-museum, perhaps with a Long John Silver theme using a variety of marine salvage. A missed opportunity?

Following our shipboard experience we would have then headed towards the Midland Hotel. This would have involved passing the Super Swimming Stadium and we probably took a peek in there. The Midland Hotel and the Super Swimming Stadium were two of the resort's most important assets – for completely different reasons. Their only similarity was that they were both clinically white. The Hotel was Morecambe's most architecturally significant building, while the *Lido* had been the costliest, yet most popular enterprise. It had been opened by the President of the LMS Railway in 1936. Both national and international swimming events had been staged there throughout the years. This stadium was either Britain's largest, or possibly Europe's, largest open-air swimming pool. It was one of the resort's proudest features (it was around this *Lido* that the Miss Great Britain beauty pageant had been inaugurated). Again, when I learned of its demise (1977), I remember thinking that it was a bad call, on the part of Lancaster County Council, not to have had it repaired – or even improved! With the modern building techniques then available, including such as concrete pumping, was it such an insurmountable problem?

Arriving at the *Midland* we would head for the *Seahorse Bar* (post Millennium the Rotunda Bar). There, we would sit at a table outside whilst John, the oldest and tallest, went inside to get the drinks. For about thirty minutes, as well as our beer, we would sit drinking in the view. Following our swift half, we headed next for the Winter Gardens Fairground. Crossing back over Marine Road, we would stop for hot dogs (hot dogs being the only available [hot] street food at that time).

Access to this fairground was either through the Winter Gardens Arcade, between Littlewoods and Woolworths, or through the passage at the side of the Winter Gardens Ballroom. A little used point of entry, not generally used by fun-seekers, was *via* Bath Street. This was off Northumberland Street next to the Bath Hotel. The Winter Gardens Fairground was favoured by families with younger children. The rides were somewhat smaller and the *clientele* less rowdy than at the Pleasure Park. The most thrilling ride was the Mouse.[10]

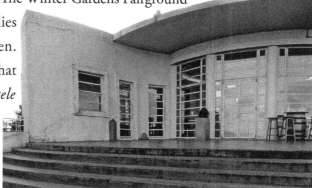
The entrance to the Seahorse Bar (Rotunda Bar).

Other rides and attractions included a carousel (galloping horses); the Harris family's laughing clowns; a rather 'naff' ghost train; smaller round-abouts for kiddies and a wonder waltzer. We tended to congregate around the Waltzer – probably because of the latest pop records blurting-out from loud speakers! Gone were the days of fairground *Gavioli* organs. With the advent of sixties pop music it was all that teenagers wanted to hear. Records by the Beatles (*I Saw Her Standing There*); Rolling Stones (*I Can't Get No Satisfaction*); Gerry and the Pacemakers *(How Do You Do It?)* and Cilla Black (*Anyone who had a Heart*), could be heard everywhere. One record in particular that seemed to be played incessantly was *The Night Has a Thousand Eyes* by Bobby Vee!

We tended to stay at this fairground until it was time to catch our train home. *(This fairground site, from the mid-eighties, became the location of a very popular Sunday Market)*. On later visits, by which time we were older, we joined the resort's night life. During one of our visits the Stones were scheduled to appear at the Winter Gardens. We had eagerly joined the throng

---

10 The Mouse: I had ridden on this in 1959/60 at the Winter Gardens Fairground. It was a spine-chilling, white knuckle, experience. I recall it being very jerky with sharp turns on its upper level. Because of this it was not popular with young families so it may have been dismantled and resited at the West End Pleasure Park and renamed Wild Mouse.

of young people who were queuing outside of the theatre. As there seemed to be a delay in the group arriving, the crowd became rowdy and impatient and so the local police decided, in the interest of public order, to cancel the event. We all had to disperse. Dejected, we headed for the *Tivoli Bar*. The *Tivoli Bar* on West View Terrace provided live music (local groups) but you had to queue outside to get in. Entry was controlled by a bouncer. I recall the packed interior being claustrophobic. It had a low ceiling and virtually no windows. Being asthmatic, I didn't stay long in there.

Moving on, we made for Queen Street which, during the period being recalled, was known as the Barbary Coast. It was a drinker's paradise! One of the houses recalled is: *The Queens Hotel,* which stands at the corner of Marine Road and Queen Street. It was the only pub on this street that we never managed to access. It operated a very strict under-age policy! I recall the exterior and the large, neon-lit letters – OBJ. *'Oh Be Joyful',* advertising Dutton's English Ales, the 'O' encircling a smiley face! Built in 1840 the Queens, at 274 Marine Road Central, is a Grade II Listed Building. Next along was the *Masons* and then the *Bradford Arms,* which always hosted a local beat group. Across the street was the *Joiners Arms*. This and The Ship, were the only houses on our patch that sold Yates and Jackson's beer. The pint glasses, although still the beer mug style, were not the ubiquitous dimpled type. The *Joiner's* ale was served in a sort of polygonal beer mug. *The Bull* was farther down and just off Queen Street, being on Lines Street. Our first port of call would have been the *Palatine* at 1, The Crescent.

Almost opposite the *Queens* and near the clock tower was the entrance to Central Pier. This pier was a place we never visited during our sixties visits to the resort. It no longer looked inviting and, in any event, none of our group was interested in either wrestling or amateur dramatics. The name Archie Collis was still very prominent however and still synonymous with the piers. A hall located on the T section at the end of the pier carried a large banner bearing his name.

The Palatine; 2023: S. Henderson

The Clock Tower
Alexander P. Kapp; licensed for reuse under Creative Commonds

Archie Collis (1913-2005) was a *sand grown* comedian born near to Northumberland Street. He had a natural talent to amuse. For a while he worked at Ward's Ship Breakers at the old harbour. He had also done some boxing. He later became the manager of both piers. My uncle Frank spoke highly of him and always laughed when his *alter ego*, Nobby Clark, was mentioned.

Twenty years later, my sister and her husband moved from the Railway in Dalton-in-Furness to take over the running of the Palatine. Joan and Paul Kane ran this pub for around ten years, turning it into a popular Morecambe watering hole. There was a popular snooker hall further along the front and on the corner of Euston Road. We only knew it as Jack's. My son Paul and nephew, Simon, spent many a happy hour in Jack's. Not long after moving into the pub a tragic event occurred. Peter, a younger brother, had taken ill at 2am at his home in Barrow. He telephoned me and I took him to our local hospital where he was kept in for observation. Unable to find anything wrong, they discharged him the following day. Still not feeling well, he went to Morecambe to stay with Joan and her family at the Palatine. The next day he started with a fit of hiccups, which persisted all the following day. Then, while on his way to bed, he seemed to have some kind of seizure. My sister said that his face seemed to implode, as if subject to some terrible external force! Peter was taken, by ambulance, to the Queen Victoria Hospital, where he, sadly, passed away. This was in late summer, 1984.

Peter had been a keen supporter of wresting. Each stay at the *Palatine* would coincide with a wrestling programme, either on Central Pier or in the Winter Gardens Ballroom. Among his wrestling heroes were Big Daddy and Mick McManus.

Having completed our cruise of the Barbary Coast, by which time it would be early evening, we made for the West End Pleasure Park. On this return journey we would make our way along Back Crescent Street, then along Victoria Street turning at Brubecks and back onto the front. Passing in front of the Promenade Station, we crossed the forecourt of Fahy's Garage. Fahy's, as well as being a garage, was also a used car saleroom (mainly for the popular Mini). It was also a convenient car parking area for visitors who had arrived in Morecambe by road.

Hiccups death shock

A POPULAR Barrow man has died in hospital at Morecambe where he was recuperating after being discharged from North Lonsdale Hospital.

Vickers' cleaner Peter John Henderson, 21, of Abattoir Cottage, Cavendish Street, Barrow, died in the resort's Queen Victoria Hospital.

He was admitted after being taken ill with a severe bout of hiccups while staying with his sister Mrs Joan Kane, w h o manages the Palatine Hotel, Morecambe.

His family has been told that a postmortem revealed his death was due to natural causes and there will not be an inquest.

His death left the family stunned especially since, although slightly retarded, he had not had an illness in his life.

His elder brother, Mr Stanley Henderson, of Buller Street, Walney, said: "The doctor thought he was suffering from 'flu but about 2 a.m. last Monday he was worse and I took him to hospital.

"He was admitted by 2 a.m. and was kept in until Wednesday when he was discharged with antibiotics, but he had not eaten for a week."

He went to Morecambe to recuperate, only to be taken ill again.

Mrs Kane, his sister, said: "He took some sort of fit on the stairs here so we rushed him to hospital.

"We have been told that it was natural causes, although we have not yet been given the precise cause of death but I think it may have been something cerebral.

"I think it was possibly something that could have happened sooner or later.

"Peter was very independent and had a wonderful social life and was very well-known in the town," she said.

He had worked at Vickers for some years as a cleaner in the engineering works and he also carried out other duties.

The funeral takes place in Barrow next Tuesday.

The main building had a barrel-shaped roof and the words **'Fahy's Garage'** were emblazoned on this roof in large, white lettering (possibly for the benefit of those arriving by helicopter?).

Having walked past the garage, we came next to the *Empire Complex*. This had opened in 1939/40. It comprised the Empire Cinema, the Floral Hall, the Arcadia Cinema and Restaurant, also Lunn's Shopping Arcade. Although possibly the hub of Morecambe's evening activity, it was somewhere we never explored (regrettably). The Floral Hall, with its sprung floor of Canadian maple, was *the* destination for dancers! There were other places in Morecambe to dance. Dancing at the *Floral* was *de rigueur*. Almost everyone danced during the period of my recall, including my parents, uncles and aunts and all their friends. The *Floral's* large interior, I am told, had a decorative brilliance! It was in an *art nouveau* style which included the lavish use

of chromium with huge chandeliers. There was a large revolving Addenbroke[11], kaleidoscopic glitter ball. For the non-dancers and spectators there was a 50-foot balcony bar. The Floral Hall was, indeed, a *palais de danse* second to none!

Immediately next door to this green and cream temple of jollity was West End Pleasure Park and the mighty Cyclone – our intended destination.

A year or so later, when ballroom dancing had declined in popularity, groups of older lads came regularly from Barrow to the Floral Hall. Inevitably fights would erupt between the Morecambe and the Barrow guys. By 1968 Morecambe's premier dance venue had gone over to bingo (the last dance on Central Pier was in November, 1970).

---

11 Harold Rupert Vivian Addenbroke aka Mr Morecambe, had been manager of the Tower, later the Gaumont (Dem. 1959/60). His Kaleidoscopic Glitter Globe had been one of Morecambe's greatest inventions – *Bingham*.

The Pleasure Park occupied a 10-acre site. During the early days of the resort this site had been a railhead, serving as a storage area between the railways and the harbour. Early maps[12] clearly show a large laundry, a drying shed, goods sheds and a cattle siding, together with stock pens. At the site that would later be occupied by the Empire Complex, was a mound known as Rabbit Hill. This was topped with a putting green. The fairground started from a small focus, expanding until it eventually occupied the whole 10-acre site. At one point the Figure of Eight ride, courtesy of Messrs Helter, shared the site with the cattle pens and sidings. Over the decades, this place of mirth and merriment has been known as: The Figure of Eight Park; Morecambe Pleasure Park; West End Pleasure Park; Fun City and finally, Frontierland.

The Morecambe Cyclone had been designed originally as *Le Cyclone* for the *Paris Internationale Exposition of 1937*. It had been engineered by an American firm (Traver's Engineering). Harry Traver was renowned for his work on early roller coasters and similar rides. His roller coasters became legendary for their thrilling swooping turns and twists. The most famous were his Cyclone Safety Coasters, erected throughout the USA and Canada. From glimpses of the ride's configuration at the Paris location, it is clear that several modifications would have been required to make it fit the Morecambe site, where it was installed in 1939.

The Cyclone was constructed almost entirely of timber and, at the time, was painted brilliant white. It could be seen from almost anywhere along the front, from the Battery to the Midland! It was, in effect, Morecambe's *Big One*. Next to this was the big wheel. Opposite was a curved row of fairground stalls, i.e. a rifle-range; coconut shy; hoop-la and a stall where you threw darts at rows of playing cards for a choice of soft-toy prizes. Towards

---

12 Maps: 6 inch O/S Maps, 1901 and 1913.

the rear of the park was a dedicated area for children's rides. Eagerly, we would join the Cyclone's queue. The ride started with a 180° turn around a semi- circular façade and then onto the *hill lift* up to the high-point. During the slow haul to the top I can recall hearing the click-click of the ride's ratchet safety mechanism. Also, having achieved a certain altitude, various unattractive features of the resort came into view! Clearly visible were all the dustbins to the rear of the Empire Complex, probably belonging to the Arcadian Restaurant? The main vista from our vantage point was the large area of redundant railway sidings, overgrown with weeds, probably reaching back to the days of Morecambe Harbour. Additionally, the up and down tracks of Promenade Station, curving away into the distance. The trees visible were all that remained of *Sloethorne Wood*. Also clearly visible were allotment gardens and pigeon coups to the rear of some boarding houses off West End Road. Approaching the ride's high-point, we passed under a warning sign stating that it was dangerous to stand up. Then, as the train of cars rolled slowly around the curve, our grip would tighten on the safety bar, and then Whoosh! We were off to the races!! Our thrilling ride – at just under one kilometre - ended near to our start-point at a position known as the Station where we would usually be offered a second go for half-price. Upon alighting, we would then make our way to the Oyster Bar. This was a kiosk near to the centre of the park, next to the big helter-skelter. There, we would gorge on whelks which were a particular favourite. Also available were cockles and Baxter's shrimps. Other rides recalled are the Octopus, Wild Mouse and maybe a go-kart circuit? Depending upon the scene[13], we may have stayed longer or we may have headed west for *Davy Jones' Locker*.

---

13 The 'scene' referred to alluded to the social scene and whether there was any talent about (mini-skirted young things). During the period under review Mary Quant's mini skirt had just arrived. The decade saw a kind of teen revolution. Young people, hitherto the children of a structured parental society, started to demand a say in how they lived their lives in terms of fashion, music and hairstyles. It is interesting to note that when the Beatles broke onto the music scene, they were, initially, more of a sensation because of their hairstyles!

View of West End Pleasure Park during 1960s.
Morecambe & Heysham Past and Present (D. Wharfedale).

View of West End Pleasure Park in 1996, by which time it was Frontierland. Go-karts and part of the Cyclone can be seen.
Photo courtesy of John Goodings.

This was a cellar bar located in the basement of the Clarenden Hotel. It was a popular evening meeting place for our age-group.

Whilst in that area we would invariably head further along the front to the waxworks (*Tussaud Exhibition*). This had been established in an old cinema, the Whitehall Cinema, the resort's first picture palace that had closed in 1955 - according to the besmocked curator who took our entrance fee. The wax figures on display were amazing! Depictions of celebrities such as film stars, sporting heroes and politicians. The interior of the museum, with its fake cobwebs and subdued lighting, was eerie. It was not a place I would have liked to visit alone. It is strange how a person can be brave when in the company of friends. Towards the back of the museum was a separate area which carried a warning about material that may cause distress! In this section were depictions of torture, surgical procedures, e.g. amputations and people afflicted with advanced venereal disease (syphilis etc.), as well as a variety of teratomatous excrescences. I recall the most freakish exhibit in this area was the sexual *bits* of a hermaphrodite. The waxworks was the farthest west that we would venture in those days. It would be ten years before I visited the West End proper.

After several Morecambe visits I suppose it was inevitable that we would eventually start to deviate from our routine and explore the hinterland. On one particular Saturday, having completed our crawl of the Barbary Coast, we turned left at the bottom of Queen Street into Deansgate and onto Poulton Road where we stumbled, to our sheer delight, on a place called the *Smugglers Den*! This establishment, the town's oldest pub, was only a Yorkshire pudding's throw from the market on Poulton Square.

One of my sources told me that, as far back as the 1880s, a market was opened on Victoria Street. It was a wooden, single-storey building which had a brick clock tower over its main entrance. Unfortunately, one night in 1884 it burned to the ground. Some ten years later, another market, Queen's Market, sprung up on the site (as I write this book, the building, which has also been the Palladium Cinema and a night club, is being lovingly restored by a Morecambe plumber, Nick Smith, who has established a Community Interest Company to further his aim).

The interior of the *Smugglers Den* was laid out just how you would expect the archetypal smugglers' cache to be. (Shouldn't the below decks area of the Moby Dick have been on a similar theme?). There was also a large and inviting coal fire – which tells me that our visit to Morecambe on that occasion must have been late in the season - possibly autumn. Fired with renewed enthusiasm we moved on, heading back to the Euston Road area where we would pause to look at several quirky little shops. These shops catered for collectors; model makers and others with special interests. I recall one in particular displayed model stationary steam engines. Moving on and getting back onto Market Street and then Victoria Street we next turned onto New Street. Directly ahead of us at the bottom of New Street was a British Legion

The Smugglers Den; 2023: *S. Henderson Collection.*

Club. The club, at 31 Edward Street, was in a large sandstone building with mullioned windows. We made an entrance and signed the visitors' book. The patronage appeared to be mainly elderly gentlemen (probably ex-servicemen) who made us all welcome. To cut to the chase, our visit was spent playing snooker, cards (Welch Don) and darts. After a totally unex-

pected and enjoyable evening, we made our exit, bidding our hosts farewell and literally running for the last train back to Lancaster, in the hope of catching the *Whip* (this was the last train to Barrow, which departed Lancaster Castle Station at 11pm.).

Edward Street comprises, along its east side, a terrace of two-storey, bay-windowed houses. These houses backed onto the redundant railway sidings. Continuing along the street on our way back to the station, my interest was piqued by a rather unusual and compact church building with amazing stained-glass windows. St Laurence's Anglican Church had been designed to fit onto a tapered piece of land where Edward Street runs into Victoria Street. Sitting between Chapel Street and New Street, it appeared to have been 'squeezed in' on an unusually small footprint for an ecclesiastic building. Research in later years revealed that the architectural historian, Pevsner, had said it was the best church in Morecambe to have been designed by the Lancaster architects, Paley and Austin. It was designated a Grade ll listed building in 1979. During a fact-finding visit to Morecambe, while researching this book, I went to look at Morecambe's best church, only to find that it is now redundant with its magnificent windows covered over (what was to become of the organ?). It saddens me to see a House of God lying fallow, an all too familiar sight post Millennium. Over the years, this

31 Edward Street; 2023: This building has had several uses over the years, including being the Royal British Legion Club. *S. Henderson Collection.*

St Laurence's Church (C of E); 2023. The building has, or had, stained-glass windows made by the Lancaster firm Shrigley and Hunt, also Abbott & Co. of London and Lancaster. It is a Grade II Listed Building. List Entry: 1292956.

building would have witnessed moments of poignancy, also many happy occasions: weddings; confirmations and Christenings (Baptisms) etc.

Our last visit of '63 would have been to see the switching on of the Lights. A jazz musician called Bernard Stanley Bilk, better known as Acker Bilk, had the privilege on this occasion. The big switch-on took place in Happy Mount Park. It really was a spectacle and something I will always remember! Our visit on the reference occasion, however, wasn't primarily to Morecambe. It was an outing of the Barrow *AFC*

Acker Bilk in the 1960s *CC BY-SA 3.0*

Supporters' Club to a venue in Carnforth called Warton Grange. It was preceded by a drive along Morecambe's four-mile front to view the Illuminations and then back to Carnforth. Warton Grange was a kind of country hotel. It was a popular venue during the sixties for outings from working men's clubs and the like. There were snooker tables and facilities for other pub games. A sit-down meal, followed by an evening's entertainment was the standard fare.

Another experience involving Morecambe's illuminations, if the reader will indulge me, went as follows: It was in 1958, if memory serves, and I was playing in our back street with two friends. A man I will refer to as Walter, a neighbour, had just taken delivery of his first motor car, a black Ford Popular. Walter was a single man. He had lived in our street all his life, in fact he had been to school with my father. Walter approached us and asked if we would like a run out in his new car to see Morecambe's Lights. Overjoyed, we all ran indoors to seek our mothers' permission – which was unanimously given. I recall having a quick bath and then donning my Sunday school clothes, then rushing to Walter's house where my two friends awaited. After waving goodbye, we set off. The road out of Barrow is the A590 which runs all the way to the Levens (around 30 miles), where it joined the A6 at a lights-controlled junction. However, after only ten minutes or so into our journey Walter turned off the main road onto a country lane which led to a village called Urswick. Walter wasn't a talkative individual, I think the word taciturn would have described him. "Where are we heading?" I remember asking. "You'll see", replied our chauffeur. I knew I would *see* but this wasn't the way to Morecambe! We turned left into the village and then, after crossing a cattle grid, the road took an upward turn onto an area of common land known as Birkrigg. I had been there before. It was a local beauty spot, the highest ground on Low Furness, being around 450feet above sea-level. It offered a 360° view of the surrounding area. Walter brought his jalopy to a stop at an appropriate place and turned off the engine. Bewildered, we looked at each other. "What now?" we enquired of our tour guide. "Just be patient and keep looking yonder, across the bay", he replied. It must have taken ten or fifteen minutes and we were becoming fidgety. Suddenly the spectacle unfolded! Like a diamond necklace being drawn slowly from a black velvet bag, the illuminations came on, twinkling away in a variety of colours! "There you are!" announced Walter – "Morecambe Lights!" and what a sight to behold too! I recall noticing that other cars were parking-up near to us for the same reason. Walter produced a large Thermos flask and a parcel of banana sandwiches, which we shared.

I suppose our initial reaction was one of disappointment. We were all under the impression that we were being taken to Morecambe, although Walter had never said as much. And so, on that balmy evening in October, we enjoyed Morecambe from a distance!

Arriving home later that evening, my dad asked how Morecambe was. I would have replied grand.

"Morecambe was grand - Grand as 'owt!"

CHAPTER FIVE

Further Back in the Day

Acollection of colourised photographs from the Sankey Family
Phographic Collection. Courtesy of Cumbria Archives and Local
Studies Centre (Barrow).

GRAND HOTEL, EAST END, MORECAMBE.

The Grand Hotel. This edifice, for me personally, was Morecambe's most imposing building. It had been
advertised as 'The largest and most artistic hotel in Morecambe'. Located on Marine Road on the corner of
Thornton Road, it was demolished in 1989. Sankey Ref: 4967. (A brief description of its sumptuously rich interior
can be found in Bingham's comprehensive history of Morecambe – Lost Resort?).

Euston Road Station in the days of the London & North-Western Railway. Opened in 1886 as Morecambe Station, with five platforms, renamed Morecambe Euston Road Station in 1924; closed 1963. Sankey Ref: 6294.

Eidsforth Terrace, Marine Road, East. Morecambe's Tower is to the left. Sankey No: 4958.

Mayor Birkett's Grandfather Clock in the area once known as Poulton Green.
It is a Grade II Listed Building.List Entry No. 1279837. Sankey Ref: 4978.

The original Midland Hotel, built in 1847 as the North-Western Hotel. Sankey Ref: 4976.

Central Pier. Note the 'Taj Mahal', Pavilion. Sankey Ref: 6292.

West End Pier. Sankey Ref: 6295.

Winter Gardens Entertainment Complex, looking east. The complex originated with the building of the Oriental Ballroom, also known as the People's Palace, in 1878. The theatre (which still stands), was originally the Victoria Pavilion, built in 1897. After the death of Queen Victoria they were renamed the King's Pavilion and the Empress Ballroom. The surviving building, which closed in1977, is a Grade II listed building. List Entry: 1025280. To the left of the image a horse-drawn tram heads east along Marine Road. *Sankey Ref: 6299. Caption Courtesy of English Heritage.*

RMS Majestic in Morecambe Harbour. Note the old rail terminus and lighthouse on the Stone Jetty (right). The vessel was here for breaking-up. Majestic was a White Star liner of 10,000 gross tons. She was launched at Harland and Wolff, Belfast in 1889; claiming the Blue Riband on a return journey from New York. Majestic was retired in 1912 when Titanic entered service. Following the tragic loss of Titanic, the Majestic was brought back into service to resume her former role. She was bought, in 1914, by Ward for scrapping. Sankey Ref: 4996.

The Alhambra Palace (Jewel of the West End) C.1910; the suited gentlemen to the left of the photo are at the entrance to West End Pier. Sankey Ref: 4983.

Coming Home on Saturday... with some from ROCK Morecambe

Appendix

Winter Gardens

The Winter Gardens had supplanted the earlier Summer Gardens which had been on Regent Road, at the site where Regent Park currently stands. I never managed to enjoy the interior of this grandiose theatre during the period covered by this book. There was a missed opportunity to see the Rolling Stones there in 1963. This apart, my friends and I had no desire to visit.

Poster advertising the Minstrels at the Winter Gardens.
Courtesy of Morecambe Heritage Centre.

The theatre was probably not our scene in those far off days. Ten years later, however, it was a different matter? Along with many others from Barrow I recall taking my young family to see the spectacular Black & White Minstrel Show (every seaside resort in those days featured the show on the back of the immensely popular TV version that had won the prestigious *Golden Rose of Montreux* award.

At our visit in the summer of '74, the auditorium of Morecambe's grandest theatre was pleasantly full! I had been in the New York Winter Garden Theatre. Its auditorium does not compare with that of Morecambe.

The Winter Gardens in 2023 courtesy of Russell Holden

Since its closure in 1977 a campaign for the theatre's restoration began in 1986 when the Friends of the Winter Gardens was formed.

They established a charitable trust company called The Winter Gardens Preservation Trust (www.morecambewintergardens.co.uk). The old building has an exciting future.

Arson?

The Resort must have been a loss adjuster's nightmare?

In view of the many assets damaged or lost due to fires over the decades, I have to ask, did the resort foster families of arsonists? Some things just appear to be beyond the bounds of chance! The Alhambra and Moby Dick for instance, both having the same owner and both catching fire contemporaneously in June, 1970!

Among the business assets lost to fire:

Victoria Market, 1884.

Pavilion, West End Pier, 1917.

Central Pier, 1934 and 1991.

Imperial Hotel, Regent Road, 1949 (October).

Pleasure Park, 1955.

Alhambra, 1970 (June).

Moby Dick, 1970 (June).

Fun City. Damage to the value of one million pounds! 1986.

Mega Zone, 2014 (June).

Joy's Toys, Albert Street, 2016.

Frontierland (Ranch House, go-karts etc.) 1997 (July).

Gordon Club, 2019.

Success is looming for top student. (p.7)

Top textile student Nigel Clayton was all dressed up with the praise of industry chiefs ringing in his ears at a Morecambe factory.

For the 22 year-old loom overlooker with crepe bandage manufacturers, Creban Ltd. on the White Lund Industrial Estate, won first place in the region for his exam results at Blackburn Technical College.

Nigel, of Westgate, Morecambe, who has been with Creban since he left school six years ago, has worked his way up the ladder from trainee. Company personnel training manager Derek North said: 'From our point of view Nigel is a great success. He has worked very hard and has long-term career prospects. I am very pleased. There is reason for faith in the textile industry.

Nigel received his award as top student and a £25 cheque from Mr Bernard Smith, director of J. R. and A. Smith of Preston, who is also chairman of the North Lancashire and Cumbria Textile Employers Association.

Nigel, an ex-Heysham High School pupil who plays in goal for Carnforth Rangers, was surprised when he heard of his award from shift supervisor Jack Parkinson.

Said Nigel: 'I am amazed and very pleased. The first I knew about this was only a fortnight ago'. The workforce at Creban have a second reason for celebrating. Their largest shipment – 14,000 dozen bandage packs in two containers – is on its way to an Australian hospital this week. *Lancashire Post.*

Acknowledgements and Permissions

Grateful thanks are extended to everyone who has contributed in any shape or form to this book. The author is also deeply indebted to the following: Patricia Stockton, for sharing her memories and for making available her father's collection of Morecambe and Ribble Bus Ephemera.

Anthony Stuart Booth; Janet Clayton; John Goodings; Barrie Marshall; Susan Sullivan and Damien Wharfedale of Morecambe and Heysham Past and Present.

Morecambe Heritage Centre: (Peter Wade; Debbie Cain; Sue Nelson and Christine Stebbing).

A special thank-you is extended to Susan Benson, archivist at Cumbria Local Studies Centre (Barrow), for granting permission to use images from the Sankey Family Photographic Collection.

Finally a massive thanks to Russell Holden of Pixel Tweaks Publications for once again working his magic!

All possible care has been taken to trace the rights holders of images and for some of the texts quoted. If there are any oversights, credits can be added to future editions, following a request in writing to the publisher.

Publications Consulted

Roger K. Bingham; *Lost Resort? - The Flow and Ebb of Morecambe (1990)*.

Madeleine Bunting; *The Seaside - England's Love Affair (2023)*.

Lancaster Guardian (Inc. Morecambe Visitor).

Ribble Motor Services; *Staff Bulletins (various dates)*.

Websites

Morecambeology

Morecambe & Heysham Past and Present.

Lostlidos.com

Seasidehistory.co.uk

Attributions

Beauty Surrounds, Health Abounds: Morecambe's motto. In the year 1925 a competition was organised to see who could come up with an appropriate motto for the resort. The winner was a Mr J. Robinson, a greengrocer of Back Crescent Street, Morecambe.

England's Coastline is a national Treasure David Milliband (2007)

Its great pablum in Pablo's: John Baker.

I like Morecambe. I'm not at all sure why, but I do: Bill Bryson.

The English invented the seaside. God created Morecambe: Hannah E. Henderson.

I'nt it great to be daft? Albert Modley.

Blackpool: a great roaring spangled beast – J.B. Priestly.

If you spend the evening you'll want to stay, watching the sunset on Half Moon Bay: Old Cape Cod (excerpt). A 1957 million-selling song based on a poem by C. Rothrock.

If you like the taste of a lobster stew, served by a window with an ocean view. (Old Cape Cod).

Moby Dick (Ryelands) history: P. Wade

Glossary

Eidsforth: one of Morecambe's earliest families. They lived at Poulton Hall.

Lido: an Italian word (pronounced Leedo). Literal meaning: a sandbank. Adopted, from 1860, to mean public open-air swimming pool and its immediate surroundings.

Railway Station: this is the correct nomenclature for a place in the UK where you catch a train. In recent years the unofficial term 'Train Station' seems to be creeping into usage.

Resort: a coastal town visited by many to enjoy its beach and attractions

Sand Grown 'Un: a person born in Morecambe.

The Author

Stan Henderson is a Cumbrian senior citizen born in 1949. He was born, reared and schooled in Hindpool, Barrow-in-Furness. His industrial life was spent largely in the drawing offices of Vickers Shipbuilders (later VSEL), Barrow where he held a management grade, senior staff position. For several

years, during the 1970s, Stan was a part-time lecturer at Barrow College of Further Education. In 1995 he took voluntary redundancy, leaving the shipyard to run a large convenie nce store with his family on Walney Island. Since attaining retirement age he has written several books including three on Barrow Steelworks which he co-authored with local photographer, Ken Royall. The books are sold in support of the Emergency Services. He now spends most of his time at a holiday park in Haverigg, South Lakes.

Stan & Ollie (his great grandson).

Also by the author ...

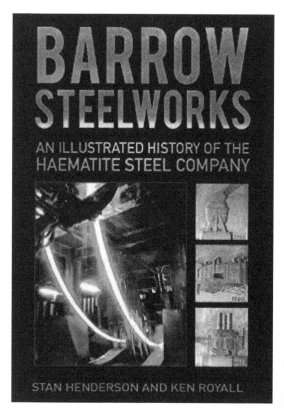

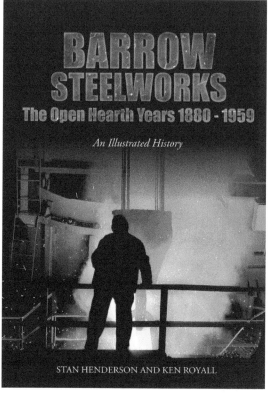

During the second half of the nineteenth century, Barrow-in-Furness became a pioneer in iron and steel production. It went on to grow astronomically – owning collieries in three counties and ore mines in two – and became the largest integrated steelworks in north Lancashire and Cumberland and, at one time, the largest steelworks in the world. Its success was due, in part, to having the prestige of three dukes as directors, as well as to being only 2 miles away from one of the largest and richest iron ore mines in the country.

The 1880s were a decade of change for Barrow works with some of the main players departing the scene. The arrival of the basic method of steelmaking, took away the lucrative position held by the directors and shareholders who had drained the coffers leaving virtually nothing for re-investment. After the Great War the company was limping along. The evacuation of Dunkirk at the start of WWII together with the blocking of special steels produced a demand for the kind of steel the making of which Barrow was a past master. Under United Steel's banner Barrow would see security of employment.

Paperback: 160 pages
Publisher: The History Press;
Language: English
ISBN-13: 978-0750963787

available at
amazon

Paperback: 98 pages
Publisher: Stanley Henderson
Language: English
ISBN-13: 978-0995619050

available at
amazon

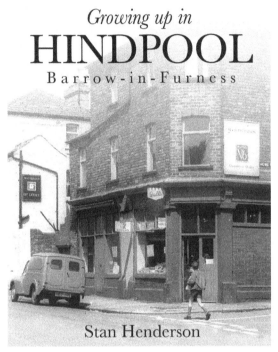

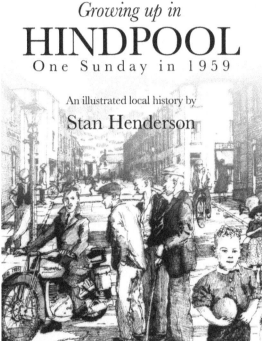

The history of Hindpool has been likened to a patchwork quilt, with each fragment, or patch, different in time, size, shape and colour. In his book the author has woven his quilt with the thread of family history and personal experience. The story starts with the arrival in Barrow of the writer's ancestors, immigrants from Shropshire, who had come to work on the blast furnaces of the local, monster, Ironworks. These works would later hold an unexplained fascination for the author, who, in this book takes the reader on a conducted tour around the historic works.

In this follow-up to Growing Up in Hindpool, the author completes his patchwork quilt with respect to the industries, institutions and businesses to which he has been directly or indirectly involved. The reader is taken on a walk out of the district and, via Lower Cocken, into Ormsgill, then back into Hindpool. During this walk, which 60-years ago, was undertaken at least once per week, the author reflects upon aspects of 1950's life, bygone industries, landmarks and some of the local characters that made Hindpool one of Barrow's most fascinating places in which to belong.

Paperback: 140 pages
Publisher: Stanley Henderson
Language: English
ISBN-13: 978-1916021747

available at
amazon

Paperback: 84 pages
Publisher: Stanley Henderson
Language: English
ISBN-13: 978-1916275836

available at
amazon

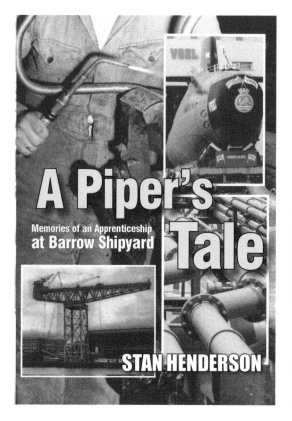

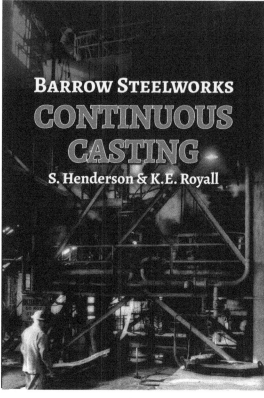

A Pipers Tale records the impressions made on a teenager as he makes his way into the thorny world of shipbuilding. A world in which the author, during the 1960s, witnessed the change from traditional shipbuilding, where vessels were constructed with a minimum, but adequate, level of technical support via long established trade practices and skills, to the cutting-edge of science-based projects as the Yard at Barrow became a 'Leader in Marine Technology' with the making of sophisticated warships and first-of-class vessels. Saluting the the wealth of characters and personalities that comprised the Yard's Plumbing Fraternity.

Paperback: 96 pages
Publisher: Stanley Henderson
Language: English
ISBN-13: 978-0995619081

available at
amazon

Since the end of the Second World War (1939-1945), there have been some outstanding technical developments in steelmaking, which have since been adopted on a worldwide basis. These developments include the use of oxygen in bulk; automation; high-speed rolling and continuous casting. During the 50s & 60s, the works at Barrow adopted all four initiatives in varying degrees. Most notable for us was the development of High-Speed Continuous Casting. In this book the authors are attempting to lay down a permanent record of what was achieved locally and thereby, hopefully, preserving the memory of a once-proud industry.

Paperback: 88 pages
Publisher: Stanley Henderson
Language: English
ISBN-13: 978-1913898243

available at
amazon

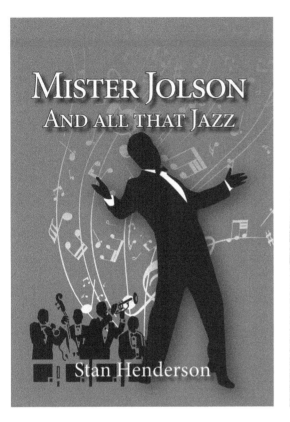

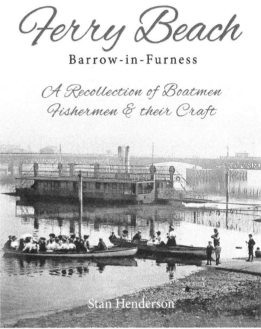

In this book, which is an appreciation of the popular art, the author takes us on a fleeting excursion through the evolution of 'pop' - from ragtime to hot jazz and in to the swing era - a fascinating insight into the early Broadway Musical and the birth of the 'talkies'.

The emergence of the Great American Song Book, and the influence of Al Jolson's career on popular singing; his relationship with the principal song writers, and how he inspired the great vocal stars who followed, including Ethel Waters, Bing Crosby, Judy Garland and Frank Sinatra.

Ferry Beach is a captivating recollection of the men and boats that have sailed the waters around Barrow-in-Furness for generations. Through personal anecdotes and historical research, author Stan Henderson paints a vivid portrait of the boatmen who braved the waves, wind, and tides to make their living on the sea. Ferry Beach explores the many types of craft that have graced the waters off Barrow and is a tribute to the people who crewed them - the hardworking, skilled, and often colourful characters who kept the maritime traditions of the region alive. It offers a glimpse into a world that has largely disappeared.

Paperback: 92 pages
Publisher: Stanley Henderson
Language: English
ISBN-13: 978-1913898045

available at
amazon

Paperback: 72 pages
Publisher: Stanley Henderson
Language: English
ISBN-13: 978-1913898731

available at
amazon

Milton Keynes UK
Ingram Content Group UK Ltd.
UKHW020403240624
444489UK00005B/21